Money Matters

A Young Parent's Workbook for Finances—and the Future

This workbook is dedicated to all young parents who strive to be the best parents they can be. We honor the participants in the Meld for Young Moms and Meld for Young Dads programs for their commitment to their children, for their desire to learn and grow as parents, and for their support of each other.

A special thanks to the Minnesota Mutual Foundation for their funding support of this project.

MONEY MATTERS

was developed and published by

Staff

Victoria Hosch

Sherry Wendelin

Ann Walker Smalley

Editor

Raymond D. Kush

Cover Art

Mary Beth Berg

Meld ◆ 219 North Second Street, Suite 200
Minneapolis, MN 55401

612-332-7563 ◆ 612-344-1959 (fax)
info@meld.org ◆ www.meld.org

© **Meld 2002.** All rights reserved.
No part of this book may be reproduced
in any form without the permission of Meld.

The information in this book is true and complete to the best of our knowledge. This book is intended only as a guide. All recommendations are made without guarantees on the part of the authors. The authors and publisher disclaim all liability in connection with the use of this information.

MONEY MATTERS

A Young Parent's Workbook for Finances—and the Future

Table of Contents

It's All About Money .... page 1
Setting Financial Goals

Dollars and Sense .... page 15
Taking Control of My Money

Smart Money .... page 45
Keeping on Top of My Money and Records

It's All About Money

Setting Financial Goals

Money makes the world go 'round.
Money doesn't grow on trees.
A penny saved is a penny earned.
Spending money like water
Money isn't everything.
Money can't buy love.
The "golden rule"—he who has the gold makes the rules.

You've probably heard these and many more. There's no getting around it—money can be a big deal!

It seems everybody needs and wants money. As a parent, you need money to take care of your family. As a young parent, you may not always think you have enough money to do this. But, with a little planning you can keep a grip on your money and take care of your family by setting financial goals. Being responsible about money is a part of building a strong family.

© Meld 2002 ◆ 612-332-7563

What Money Means to Me

It can seem like we are surrounded by the idea that money is everything. TV, magazines, music, other people—they all appear to be telling us that cash is what counts above all else. And then come the added pressures of taking care of a child's wants and needs! So it shouldn't be a surprise that money looms so large in our lives. With all this coming at us, it can sometimes seem difficult to separate who we are from what we have or how much money we make.

How we learn to handle our finances can tell a lot about how we see ourselves as individuals and as parents. Our choices about money often show our beliefs about raising children, what our family means to us, the traditions and customs that are important, and more. All of these beliefs become our "values." How we get our money, how we spend it, and how we save it all reflect our values.

What Money Means to Me

So, what are your financial values?

Read each of the statements in the following boxes. Check (✓) all that are true about you and how you feel about money. Then, write how much money comes from each in the space provided. You do not have to share this information with anyone else.

Where my money comes from right now:

☐ I earn what I need to support myself and my child.   _____

☐ I get the money I need for my family from government assistance (TANF, WIC, food stamps, etc.).   _____

☐ My parents support me and my child.   _____

☐ My money comes from my boyfriend/ girlfriend.   _____

☐ My child's other parent provides financial support.   _____

☐ Other sources for the money my family needs:

_____
_____
_____
_____
_____
_____

(continued)

What Money Means to Me

In the future

☐ I plan to be able to support myself and my child with no help from my parents, my boyfriend/girlfriend, the government, or other sources.
☐ I want someone else to give me money to live on.
☐ I won't ever be able to support myself and my child.
☐ My child's other parent will be contributing financially.
☐ Who knows what the future will bring?
☐ I hope to have enough money so I can help others in financial need.
☐ Other thoughts:

_____
_____
_____
_____

To me, money

☐ makes me feel good because I can buy the same stuff other people want or have.
☐ is critical! I worry unless I know I've got what my family needs to cover the basics and have something saved for an emergency.
☐ helps me get where I want my child and me to be now and in the future.
☐ is important to have so I can do a good job as I raise my family.
☐ is no big deal! I have money or I don't. I just adjust.
☐ Other values:

_____
_____
_____
_____

What Money Means to Me

If I suddenly had "extra" money, I would

- ☐ spend all the money today with no thought for tomorrow or next week.
- ☐ save the money for emergencies and for things I am planning ahead for, such as new shoes, a different place to live, a car, college, or job training.
- ☐ buy myself and my child something nice or needed and save the rest.
- ☐ pay my bills!
- ☐ give some or all of it away.
- ☐ Other beliefs:

_____
_____
_____
_____
_____

Review your responses. Did the statements help you think about your values regarding finances? Think of other ways money plays out in your life.

The first step in getting a grip on your dollars is to understand that the reasons we handle money in certain ways is often a part of our self-image and our beliefs about how life is suppose to work. Our self-image and values can work for us and help us to make adjustments to meet certain financial goals.

Looking Back

When it comes to money, most of us have been greatly influenced since childhood by the way our families and others managed their money. How those close to us managed their money influences how we look at money today. For example:

If one person managed all the money, you may think it's a one-person job, with no room for advice from another.

If your family struggled to earn enough money, you may think having money means working many long hours or having several jobs.

If your family fought about money, you may think talking about money makes people mad.

If no one talked about money, you may think money matters should be kept secret.

If you were given most of what you asked for, you may think money is easy to come by.

Looking Back

Do any of these fit your ideas about money?

Write a few words about how you look at money now. You can use these suggestions or come up with your own. You do not have to share these answers with anyone else.

My strongest memories about my family and money are...
_____
_____
_____
_____
_____

Having money in my pocket or bank account today makes me...
_____
_____
_____
_____
_____

I want money so I...
_____
_____
_____
_____
_____

(continued)

Looking Back

> *I know (or don't know) how to handle money because...*
> _____
> _____
> _____
> _____
> _____

Try to think about "why" you responded as you did to these statements. As you think back on family experiences with money, decide which had a good influence on you. How can you use that experience now?

Money and Me—Today

Everyone needs to spend money everyday—for simple things like bus fare to bigger purchases. How you manage your money now will shape your and your children's future.

What are your spending priorities today?

Think about what you would consider as your spending priorities. This list includes some things, and you can add others that are also important for you and your family.

Mark the items you can't live without or that are very, very important to you with a **1**. Those items that would be nice to have but aren't really necessary, mark as a **2**. Things you can live without or are not very important to you, mark with a **3**.

- ____ Nice place to live
- ____ Safe neighborhood
- ____ Nice furniture
- ____ CDs, tapes, sound system
- ____ Car
- ____ Brand name clothes for me
- ____ Brand name clothes for child
- ____ Cell phone or page
- ____ Computer
- ____ TV
- ____ Cable TV
- ____ Newspaper, magazines, books
- ____ Pets
- ____ Savings or stock investments
- ____ Health insurance
- ____ College/classes for me
- ____ College for my child
- ____ Going out (clubs, movies, sports events, concerts, etc.)
- ____ Paying child support
- ____ Gifts for others
- ____ New toys for my child
- ____ Sports equipment
- ____ Cigarettes
- ____ Things that make me look good (clothes, hair, jewelry, etc.)
- ____ Eating out regularly
- ____ Convenience foods (such as frozen dinners)
- ____ Paying off credit cards
- ____ Regular medical care for my family
- ____ Contributions or donations to organizations I support
- ____ Other: _____

Money and Me—Today

Once you are done, count the ones and record that number below. Then, do the same for the twos and threes.

1 (very, very important) _____
2 (not necessary) _____
3 (not very important) _____

> ***Do you have more ones (the things you can't live without) or do you have more twos (things that are nice, but not really necessary)?***
>
> _____
>
> ***What do you think your choices say about you?***
>
> _____
> _____
> _____
> _____
> _____
>
> ***What do you think this says about your financial values or situation?***
>
> _____
> _____
> _____
> _____
> _____

Spending on wants isn't bad—it's part of life. But to support your family, your spending on "wants" has to be balanced with what you and your family need and can afford right now.

Looking Ahead

Take a look at your life now and where you want you and your family to be in the future. What will it take to get there? What are your "prospects": To have the education or training you need to get a good job? Are you planning on improving your chances? What are you doing now that will improve your financial future?

Money is just one of the resources that help us get what we need—and want—to live our lives. How we spend our money has a direct effect on whether or not we meet our goals for ourselves and our children. Use your money wisely—think about your goals, financial and otherwise, for both you and your child.

Notes About the Future

Retirement—hard to imagine, isn't it?

If you are a teen parent or even in your early twenties, retirement looks—and is—a long way off. Perhaps you haven't even had a job yet, so you may not even be sure what it really means to "retire." To retire means to stop working at a regular job and begin living on retirement income: a work pension, social security, savings, stock investments, or something similar. You won't be able to retire, though, without some planning.

When you start working, start thinking about retirement. Begin by learning what you can about retirement and starting a retirement plan. Talk to your employer or banker, read books from the library, take classes through community education, talk to a union rep if you are a union member. It is never too soon to start saving for retirement. If you start right away, even with small amounts, you will be surprised by how much you will have when you are old enough to retire.

For Your Child

Something else all parents need to think about is who will take responsibility for your child if something happens to you. Think about who you want to parent and raise your child if something were to happen to you, no matter how unlikely this appears to be. Talk over your thoughts with that person and, if they agree, formalize the arrangement through a will or other legal statement. Thoroughly check over the will to be sure it clearly states how you want your money, belongings, and other financial resources to be used to best care for your child. Keep in mind that these arrangements can and should be updated or changed as needed.

Another important step is to be sure that the names of both parents are on your child's birth certificate and that parentage is formalized so that your child can be supported, if necessary, by child support payments, social security, life insurance payments, veterans benefits, inheritance, and possibly more.

Notes About the Future

These suggestions may seem overwhelming. If they do, you're not alone in feeling that way. It can help to talk with someone you trust to get answers to your questions or to help get you in touch with someone who knows about these topics. This person can help you decide what to do and how to go about doing it.

Dollars and Sense

Taking Control of My Money

Great, you say, I've got a lot of super goals and they all cost money. Now what? How do I even begin to reach the simplest goal, let alone the bigger ones? Well, the first step is to take charge of your money. Decide that **you** are going to be the one who knows about your money and how to manage it.

What Does It Take?

Taking control of your money means you know how much you have, how much you spend, and how much you save. With this information you can manage your money to take care of the needs of your family and meet your goals.

Taking control of your money is the smart thing to do. When you know about your money, you can make decisions based on real information, not on gut feelings or something else. Not knowing about your money and not making smart decisions can lead to real problems—unpaid bills, credit problems, and more. Be smart. Make sense of your money.

So, how do you take charge? There are several steps:

- Get to know your financial situation—how much you have, where it comes from, and where it goes.
- Learn budgeting skills.
- Open a checking account.
- Set up a bill paying system.
- Start a savings plan.

> Buy a calculator. They can cost as little as $5 at just about any discount store. Having one on hand will make this whole moneything easier—and more accurate.

Taking charge means you can set goals and figure out your finances so you can meet them. You will know what is realistic to do sooner or later—move out, buy a car, go to college or vocational school, send your child to college, buy a house. Making sense of your money will give you confidence that you can take care of yourself and your child.

No two families will handle money exactly the same way. Each family has different needs and make different choices about how to spend its money.

If you're confused, don't think you're the only one who doesn't quite "get it" when it comes to money. Very few people learn money management at home or even at school. Many of us have to put some effort into understanding how money works. Money mistakes can be expensive. Take time to ask questions of people who are smart about money, read about money, and pay attention to your money.

Smart About My Money

How much do you know about money in general and about your money in particular?

This quick assessment can help you figure out what you know and what you need to learn more about.

Read each statement and then rate it: a little bit, not at all, or definitely.

Circle the words/ideas you don't know so you can ask about them or look them up. Put a check mark (✓) in the box by the things you want to really work on as you begin to take control of your money.

	A little bit	Not at all	Definitely
☐ I understand the difference between necessary and unnecessary purchases for me and my child.	_____	_____	_____
☐ I have a checking account. I know how much money is in the account at any given time.	_____	_____	_____
☐ I know how to write checks and make deposits or withdrawals.	_____	_____	_____
☐ I record my checks in the check register and keep a running balance.	_____	_____	_____
☐ I can balance my checkbook at the end of the month.	_____	_____	_____
☐ I understand compound interest in a savings account.	_____	_____	_____

(continued)

Smart About My Money

	A little bit	Not at all	Definitely
☐ I use coupons when I shop, comparison shop, and watch for sales.	_____	_____	_____
☐ I make a weekly or monthly budget and stick to it most of the time.	_____	_____	_____
☐ I understand my paycheck stub.	_____	_____	_____
☐ I know how to use a calculator to add, subtract, multiply, and divide.	_____	_____	_____
☐ I understand the difference between gross pay and net pay.	_____	_____	_____
☐ I have a rainy day fund for emergencies.	_____	_____	_____
☐ I think before I spend money I hadn't planned on spending.	_____	_____	_____
☐ I am aware of budget busters such as rent-to-own shops.	_____	_____	_____
☐ I understand payroll deductions, FICA, and taxes.	_____	_____	_____
☐ I know I have to file tax returns for federal and state taxes by April 15 every year.	_____	_____	_____
☐ I can read my monthly bank statement, compare balances with my records, and make adjustments to my checking and savings accounts.	_____	_____	_____
☐ I know where I can go for help with my finances if I need it. I am not afraid to ask for help when I need it.	_____	_____	_____

(continued)

Smart About My Money

	A little bit	Not at all	Definitely
☐ I think of my child and our future when I plan my spending budget.	_____	_____	_____
☐ I keep good records of my finances and other business.	_____	_____	_____
☐ I try not to borrow or lend money to friends or family.	_____	_____	_____
☐ I do not want to be dependent on someone else to support me and my child.	_____	_____	_____
☐ I have a savings plan, including "rules" for when I can use the money.	_____	_____	_____
☐ I can figure out the savings when something is 10%, 25%, or 30% off.	_____	_____	_____
☐ I know how to plan for big purchases. I can wait for something until I can afford it.	_____	_____	_____
☐ I know where my money comes from, where it goes, and how to manage it.	_____	_____	_____
☐ I buy for value and usefulness, not for the name brand.	_____	_____	_____
☐ I take care of my health and my child's health.	_____	_____	_____
☐ I use credit cards only occasionally and I pay off the balances every month.	_____	_____	_____

(continued)

Smart About My Money

	A little bit	Not at all	Definitely
☐ I don't rush out and buy something, either for myself or my child, just because "everyone has one."	_____	_____	_____
☐ I understand that often something "used" is as good or better then something new. I may be able to buy a name brand or better quality if I buy used items.	_____	_____	_____
☐ I know I can depend on myself to take care of my family's needs.	_____	_____	_____
☐ I understand the different kinds of insurance: health, renter's, life, disability, unemployment.	_____	_____	_____
☐ I have thought about my retirement—how I will live when I no longer work a.	_____	_____	_____
☐ I know how to figure out the sales tax on the things I buy.	_____	_____	_____

© Meld 2002 ◆ 612-332-7563

Income: Where My Money Comes From

Income is the money you earn from a job or which comes to you from other sources: child support, government assistance (TANF), food stamps, etc. Understanding all the sources of your money is the first step in taking control.

Jobs and Paychecks

For most people, their job is their largest source of income. There is a great sense of accomplishment when you receive money for work you've done. Reading your paycheck can be some of the most satisfying reading you do!

When you get paid, you will receive a paycheck and a pay stub. Look at your paycheck stub. It shows you how much you earned as well as how much was taken out for taxes, benefits, and other deductions. Mistakes on pay stubs are rare but do happen, and you want to take care of them immediately. If you see something that looks wrong, talk to your payroll clerk or supervisor.

Income: Where My Money Comes From

Understanding the abbreviations and other information on your pay stub can be a challenge.

If you need help understanding your pay stub, ask someone you trust, your supervisor, or someone in the personnel department to explain it. Keep your most recent pay stubs on file to compare to your W-2 form for accuracy.

Look over these words and their definitions. Label the different parts of the sample paycheck and pay stub on the following page.

gross pay—the amount you earned before any deductions were taken out

deductions—money taken out of your pay, money withheld

net pay—the money you get to keep

pay stub—gives you the information about your pay

period ending or pay period—date pay period ended or dates for which you are being paid

rate—hourly amount or wage you are paid

current—money for one pay period

year-to-date—how much you have earned in this job so far this year

regular—normal hours you work

overtime—hours you worked over 40 per week, often at a higher hourly rate

dirdep—direct deposit means your paycheck is deposited into your bank account by your employer

non-negotiable—means this is not a check, but a record of the amount you were paid because your money was directly deposited into your bank account

FICA—money withheld for social security

fed. tax—money withheld for federal income tax

dis.—money withheld for disability insurance (optional)

state tax—money withheld for state income tax

child support—some counties or states may deduct child support payments automatically from paychecks

medical—money withheld for medical insurance (optional)

save—money withheld for savings (optional)

© Meld 2002 ◆ 612-332-7563

Income: Where My Money Comes From

Sample paycheck and pay stub

The Big Job Company
1245 Main Street
Your Town, Your State 55000

Golden Bank, Inc.
Downtown Office
Your Town, Your State 55000

45672

Date .... October 18, 2002
Amount $333.75

Pay .... Three Hundred and Thirty-three and 75/100 Dollars

To the order of .... Shanda Preston
1234 56th Street, Apt. 7
Your Town, Your State 55000

_____
Signature

045672 :098462513 135 1235

The Big Job Company **45672**

Employee No.	Employee Name	Social Security No.	Pay Period Ending
34-1468	Shanda Preston	000-123-4567	10-18-02

Earnings	Rate	Hours	Current	Year-to-date	Deductions	Current	Year-to-date
Regular	10.50	40.0	420.00	17,640.00	FICA	32.12	1,349.46
Overtime	15.75	1.0	15.75		Fed. Tax	49.87	2,094.54
					Dis.	5.90	247.80
					State Tax	10.10	424.20
					Med. Ins.	4.00	168.00
		Totals:	435.75	17,640.00		102.00	4,284.00
	Net pay this period:		333.75				

Income: Where My Money Comes From

Look at the sample paycheck and pay stub on the previous page to answer these questions.

What is the total or gross pay for this period? _____

What is the net pay? _____

Was there overtime pay? _____

How much was taken out for FICA? _____

How much federal tax has been paid year-to-date?
_____

What is the total of all deductions taken from this check?
_____

What is the hourly rate? _____

Your paycheck and pay stub may look different from this sample, but the information will be similar. Take a look at your next pay stub to be sure you understand what it says.

One thing that can be eye-opening when you first start to work is how much of your pay is deducted for taxes and other things. Keep this in mind when you are managing your money. For example, if you make $10 an hour and work 40 hours a week (which is $400 gross pay), what you actually have to spend is closer to $300 after deductions.

Income: Where My Money Comes From

How much money do you have each month?

Write down all your income sources for one month. If you receive food stamps, for example, put down their dollar value. If your income changes from month to month—maybe you baby-sit once in awhile—for example, put down an estimate of what you make each month.

Source of Income	Amount*	Day of Month Received
TOTAL MONTHLY INCOME		

*Write down your **net pay**—what you actually take home after taxes, social security, insurance, and other deductions are taken out. **Gross pay** is the amount you earned before these deductions.

Where *Does* My Money Go?

A buck for the bus, a couple of quarters for a candy bar, a pack of diapers, a Big Mac or two, and pretty soon it adds up to "real money," as they say. Put this spending along side your fixed monthly expenses for rent and other necessities and it really adds up.

Daily and Weekly Expenses

You probably spend money almost every day. Getting a handle on this spending can be hard to do, but important if you want to take control of your money. When you look at balancing your budget, you can often cut back on this daily/weekly spending.

Find a pocket-size notebook. Date the page, then as you go through your daily and weekly activities, write down how much you spend and what it is for. It can be helpful to note the time of day, where you spent money, and what was going on at the time, too. Don't include your fixed monthly bills like rent, the electric bill, etc.

It takes awhile to get into the habit of writing it all down, but it is the only way to get a real picture of what you spend. Each day, date a new page and continue keeping track. **Write everything down—any amount, no matter how small!**

After you've done this for a few weeks, take a look at what you've been spending. Are some days' amounts much more or less than others? Look back at your notebook to see what else happened that day. Was it a day you worked? Hung out with friends at the mall? Took your baby to the doctor? Bought your mom a birthday present?

Where *Does* My Money Go?

Think about your spending patterns by grouping your expenses by what you spent the money for. Put each item in a category like those listed below and add other categories that are specific to you.

	Week 1	Week 2	Week 3	Week 4	Week 5	Totals	Average*
Groceries							
Child-related (diapers, formula, toys…)							
Entertainment (movies, video rental…)							
Transportation							
Personal (jewelry, hair, nails…)							
Health & Beauty (shampoo, vitamins)							
Clothing/Shoes							
Snacks, meals out, etc.							
Books, school supplies							
Medical and dental expenses							
Laundry							
Gifts							
Other							
Other							
TOTALS							

*To figure out the average spending, add up the weekly amounts for each category and divide by the number of weeks you kept track. If you kept track for 4 weeks, you would add the four amounts for groceries and then divide by 4 to get your average weekly spending on groceries.

Add up all the totals to see how much you spent during the time you kept track.

I spent $_____

© Meld 2002 ◆ 612-332-7563

Where *Does* My Money Go?

> As a parent, one thing you've probably noticed is how expensive children are! Diapers, toys, shoes, treats, clothes, and so on all add up. As your children get older, the expenses will increase, too, because bigger clothes and shoes—as well as their entertainment and toys—often cost more. Be sure to include all your child-related spending as you track your money and plan your budget.

Monthly Expenses

Some expenses don't change from one month to the next. You pay the same amount for rent, for example, every month. Other expenses come every month, but the amount you pay varies from one month to the next—things like utilities and car maintenance. Other expenses—maybe tuition or car insurance—happen periodically, every 3 or 6 months. List all your monthly or periodic expenses here. Use an average amount for those that change from month to month.

Expense	Amount	Date Due
Rent		
Car payment		
Car insurance		
Child support		
Child care		
Tuition		
Credit card payment		
Savings		
Utilities—		
Phone		
Gas		
Electric		
Cable TV		
Clothing		
Car maintenance		
Cell phone/pager		
Medical/dental insurance		
TOTALS		

Where *Does* My Money Go?

Add your daily/weekly spending to your monthly expenses to find your total expenses.

Daily/weekly spending .... $ _____
plus +
Monthly expenses .... $ _____
equals =
TOTAL EXPENSES .... $ _____

Total Income .... $ _____
minus -
Total Expenses .... $ _____
equals =
DIFFERENCE .... $ _____

Take a look at the difference. This is what you have left after taking all your expenses from all of your income. Once you know your income and expenses, you can tell if you have enough money to meet your needs and your children's needs. Do you?

© Meld 2002 ◆ 612-332-7563

Budgeting

"On a budget" doesn't necessarily mean pinching pennies. It means that you know how much money you have and where it will be spent. A budget shows you the choices you have about spending your money. Think of it as your "spending plan"!

Creating a budget and sticking to it, while it may be hard, is the way to really get a grip on your money and where it goes. Budgets can help you

- keep your expenses in line with your income
- pay all of your expenses when they are due
- spend wisely
- start a savings plan
- get out of debt and stay out

Spending plans are good things. They help you make smart choices about how and where you spend your money. You use a budget to control your money; so money, or worrying about money, doesn't control you. Knowing about your money gives you power over your life and your future. You will know where you are and a budget can help get you where you want your family to be.

Budgeting

Start Your Budget Planning

Based on what you have learned about your expenses, decide how much you will need to put into each area. Include the following items and any other regular expenses you identified

Expenses	Week 1	Week 2	Week 3	Week 4	Week 5 as needed	Other*
Housing						
Utilities						
Groceries						
Transportation						
Savings						
Pocket Money**						
Insurance						
WEEKLY TOTALS						

*List things that come due every 3 or 6 months so you don't forget to plan for these.

**Pocket money is the "ready cash" you have to spend as you wish. Set an amount and stick to it.

Budgeting

Cash Flow — Money In & Money Out

Have you heard the term "cash flow"? It means how your money comes in and goes out and how much money you have at any one time. Your cash flow is greatest when you get paid or receive your paycheck. Low cash flow is no mystery. It happens just before your next paycheck arrives.

Managing you cash flow is part of budgeting. If you can, spread your spending over the month so you have a fairly even cash flow. This helps your money go where it needs to go, when it needs to be there.

You've done the first step in managing your cash flow—figuring out when you need money and what you need it for. The next step is figuring out *when* you must spend money to pay a bill that is due.

Using the list you created earlier of your monthly and weekly expenses, write down the day of the month each bill is due. Don't forget to include savings in your plan.

Add the monthly expenses to the averages for your weekly spending estimates. This won't be as accurate as the monthly expenses, but you can get a good idea of your spending needs each week.

To see how much money you need each week to meet your bills and living expenses, fill in the chart on the next page. Look at your income chart on page 25 to see when your money arrives. Are your expenses greater or less than the amount of money you have each week?

Budgeting

	Money In	Money Out*	Difference (+ or -)
Week 1			
Week 2			
Week 3			
Week 4			
Week 5			
TOTALS			

*Add monthly expenses and weekly averages to arrive at the amount of money out each week.

Use this information to plan how you will manage your money each week. During the weeks there is money "left over," do you need to save it for a bill due later? Or, can you put that amount into savings?

The cash flow number in the chart above is the one in the box marked Difference (+ or -). Is your cash flow a plus (+) or minus (-) amount? If it is a plus, that means you're in the black—you can pay your bills. If it is a minus number, you're in the "red"—you spend more than you take in. Now it's time to take a look at how you can balance your budget.

© Meld 2002 ◆ 612-332-7563

Balancing My Budget

Having a "balanced budget" means that your income and expenses come out even at the end of the month or you have money left over. If your expenses are greater than your income, you need to balance your budget—adjust what you spend or increase your income. Are there ways you can increase your income? Are they realistic? How long will it take to increase your income?

Take a hard look at your expenses. Go back to your daily/weekly spending diary. Look at each of the expenses and ask yourself these questions about what you are spending:

- Which expenses *can't* be cut (rent, for example)?
- What is the least amount of money my children and I can live on?
- Am I spending my money on what we need or on what we want? Mark each expenditure as a want or a need, so you can really see which is which.
- Can I cut something out of my budget or cut back on what I spend?
- What would happen if I waited on some of my spending?

Look at what you are spending. Come up with ways to cut back. If you spend a lot on transportation because you take the bus to and from work, look at how you can cut that. Does your employer offer transportation help? Are there monthly bus passes that make each ride cheaper? Can you find a car pool or a job closer to home? Can you get there by bike—and is that realistic? Cut out or reduce some "extras" until you can balance your budget.

Balancing My Budget

Budget Busters

Even the best budgets can be sabotaged by emergencies, spending choices, limited information, or incomplete planning. On the following pages are some common money traps to avoid. Figuring out how much these traps cost you can really help you make the best use of your money.

Rent-to-Own Stores

It is tempting to go out and get that big TV or washing machine when the ads are screaming "pay only $10 a week!" Before you sign, ask questions about the interest rate, how long you would need to make payments, what happens if it breaks, and about extra fees. It is easy to end up paying two or more times the real cost of the appliance because the interest rate charged to you is so high. Take a look at the following example to see what it might really mean to purchase through a rent-to-own store.

You want a new TV. The rent-to-own store has one for $350. After adding up the store's high interest rate and extra charges that would be paid off at only $10 a week, you learn that the $350 TV really would end up costing you $750.

- How many weeks would it take to pay off the rent-to-own TV at only $10 a week?

    $750 ÷ $10 = _____ weeks to pay it off

- How long would it take to save up for a $350 TV if you saved $10 a week?

    $350 ÷ $10 = _____ weeks to save $350

- How much would you *save* by waiting until you could buy the TV with cash instead of paying the high interest and extra charges from the rent-to-own store?

    $750 - $350 = $ _____ saved by paying the total cost in cash instead of purchasing through the rent-to-own store.

> Don't forget—depending on where you live, you may also need to add in the sales tax.

Balancing My Budget

Check Cashing Stores

These stores charge a fee for each check they cash. If you have a bank account you can cash a check for free (plus you can deposit your money into your account for safe keeping).

- How much money would you pay in fees if you cashed your $350 paycheck each week for a year for a 3% fee for each check?

    $350 x .03 = $ _____ paid in fees for each check
    x 52 weeks = $_____ in fees for one year

Credit Cards

Another temptation is to charge something on a credit card when you don't have the extra cash in your budget to pay for the item right away. You then end up paying the credit card bill off slowly, with high interest charges being added each month. You might justify buying something you can't pay off right away by saying, "It's on sale!"

Now, take a look at what that item will really cost if you aren't able to make the full payment that has been charged against the account. Most credit card companies charge between 12% and 17% (or more) in interest on the unpaid balance. This means that if you don't pay off the balance, you will be charged a lot in interest every month. For example: If you kept a balance of $240 over a one-year period on your credit card, you could end up paying an additional $50 in just interest during that year!

Balancing My Budget

Costly Choices

Choosing to smoke, drink, use street drugs, or engaging in similar activities—in addition to being unhealthy and/or illegal—are expensive! Another thing parents need to think about: How do these kind of choices affect my child?

- Let's look at someone who smokes cigarettes to figure out how much money they burn up in a year:

  $ per pack of cigarettes x #_____ of packs smoked per week x 52 weeks in a year = $ _____

  This is the amount of money that is burned up in one year with this choice. It's also the amount of extra money that would be available to support a family, if the choice had been to quit or not smoke cigarettes in the first place.

If you make a similar choice, figure out how much you spend on this choice over a week, month, and year. Can you afford to use up this much money? What else could you be doing with the money?

Impulse Purchases

Advertising, store displays, hanging at the mall, feeling bad—all can contribute to buying without thinking. Often we kill time by shopping or we buy something to make us feel better. "It's only a dollar or two," we think, but it does add up.

- If you spend $12 a week more than your budgeted amount for pocket money, how much would that be a month?

  $12 x 4 weeks = $_____ non-budgeted spending a month

If you find yourself making a lot of unplanned purchases, take a look at when and where you do it and try to change the circumstances. If you have a pattern of spending unplanned money while at the mall, then try not to hang out at the mall. Or, go to the mall with a clear spending limit in mind.

© Meld 2002 ◆ 612-332-7563

Balancing My Budget

Easy Credit Offers

These companies offer you a major credit card even if you have no credit or bad credit. What's the catch? These are often secured cards. The "credit" is limited to the amount of money you give them ahead of time to keep in their bank to cover anything you charge on their card. Like a savings account, you earn interest on the money in the secured account. This interest is paid to you when you close the account. "Secured" cards are okay, and may be a good option for someone trying to build credit for a mortgage, etc.

Late Fees, Bounced Checks, and Other Fees

These are real budget busters. Banks and stores can charge as much as $25 or more for any check that your account balance can't cover. Credit card companies, landlords, utility companies, and other agencies can all tack on late fees if you don't pay on time.

- Let's say your friend fell behind in keeping her checkbook balanced and bounced two checks: one to her landlord and one to the credit card company. How much in extra fees is she charged? Add the following to see the extra money your friend had to pay because of late fees and bounced check charges.

Bank's fee for bounced checks	$20 x 2 = $40
Landlord's bank fee for handling a bounced check	$25
Credit card company's fee for handling a bounced check	$30
Credit card company's late fee	$20

Balancing My Budget

Tommy, Ralph, Calvin, and Friends

Designer names, brand names, and other trendy stuff all come at a price—and usually a big one. We all seem to want at least some of these things, but take a look at just how much of it you have bought for yourself and your child. Does a child who doesn't yet walk need shoes, let alone $35 FUBU basketball shoes? Or, do you need several pairs of $50 Tommy jeans? Wouldn't one designer pair do, so you could then buy regular jeans and necessities? When buying health and beauty products, consider the cost of the national brands compared to the store brand. For the most part, soap is soap and shampoo is shampoo. How much would you save if you bought 4 bars of soap for $1 at the dollar store instead of 4 bars for $5.97 somewhere else?

- Take a few minutes to write down some things that have busted your budget. How much money would you have saved if you hadn't bought that item or bought something less expensive instead?

It's On Sale!

50% off sounds great; you're saving half of the cost of the item, right? It is good to buy things on sale, IF you need the item! If you don't need it, where is the savings? So, step back and give yourself time to think about those sale signs before they convince you to make an unnecessary purchase. Say to yourself, "I'll come back in a little while to check this out again. I might really need it, but I'll be more certain if I give myself some time to think it over.

Balancing My Budget

The Unexpected

Parking tickets, losing stuff you need to replace, missing work because of a sick child, appliance breakdowns—any or all of these can happen. Having a cushion in your budget can really keep things from becoming a mess. A $20 parking ticket might come out of the grocery money. You may lose a day or two of pay if you have to stay home because of your sick child. Have a "rainy day" fund to back you up in case of the unexpected. And try to plan ahead so you don't get caught. Arrange backup child care for the times when your child might get sick so you don't miss work.

- Look back over the last few months and list some unexpected expenses you faced. What were they and how much did they cost? What happened because of them? Could you have done anything different to be better prepared or to avoid the unexpected expenses in the first place?

Convenience

We pay for convenience. Most things that are supposed to make life "easier" often cost more. We pay more for frozen dinners than for basic groceries. Convenience stores charge more because they are small and often offer customers fewer choices. Fast-food and other restaurants are much more expensive than eating at home or taking your lunch to work or school. Of course, some conveniences make sense.

- How much is one fast-food meal for you and your child? How often do you eat at these restaurants?

  Figure out what you are spending on fast-food meals per month.

  Cost of fast-food meal(s) $ _____ x ____# of meals per week x 4 weeks = $_____ per month.

What else could you have done with that money?

Balancing My Budget

Gambling

The lottery, street corner games, sports, casinos, and other gambling are a good way to lose money. Face it—the odds are that you are going to lose. Gambling can also be addictive for some people, which can really ruin your finances, your family life, and your job.

- Figure the cost of even simple gambling. If you bought two $1 Powerball tickets for each drawing (two drawings per week), how much would you have spent in a year?

    $4 per week for tickets x 52 weeks = $ _____ spent on gambling in a year.

How did you do? Did you gain anything or did you lose your hard earned cash? If you had tucked away that much every week, what could you have done with the money instead?

Everybody's Doing It

Other people's spending shouldn't influence yours. Just because "everyone" is getting a tattoo or buying their child designer clothes or having big birthday parties, doesn't mean you have to as well! Make your own decisions about how to spend your money.

Have you spent money lately on something because "everyone" else is? What and how much?

Everyone runs into budget busters. But, if you plan and think before you spend, you can avoid many of them. Then, when a real emergency or unexpected expense comes up, you will be better able to handle it because your overall budget is under control. Just a few of these budget busters can really wreck your carefully considered spending plan. Choose a few that you have done and add up how much money you spent. For example, you may have gotten a parking ticket, bought something you didn't need, and paid a late fee or two. If you have a consumable habit, like smoking, include that. Add it all up.

Sticking to the Budget

This is the hard part—following your budget or spending plan. It takes a lot of practice and self-discipline to stick to your plan. You are the only one who can do it; no one will make you stick to the plan. You are in charge!

Here are some ideas to help you stay with it:

- Continue to write down what you spend. You might think twice or change your mind if you take a minute to write down an expense.
- Set up a plan for paying bills and pay the important bills first.
- Don't carry a lot of cash around with you. Cash has a way of getting spent.
- Carry a small calculator to figure out sale prices, price per ounce, or whatever, so you can tell if it really is a better deal.
- Stay away from places that tempt you to spend money.
- Save money every month. This will give you a cushion when you need it and will help you reach your goals.

Your ideas on helping you stick to your budget:
_____
_____
_____

Don't give up if you can't stick with your budget right away. It takes practice and effort to change spending habits.

You will need to adjust your budget if big changes happen in your life. If there is an emergency, it will affect your budget. If you get a wage increase or lose your job, you will need to figure out a new budget. But that's okay because you know how to plan a budget. You are in charge of your money.

Sticking to the Budget

> Living on less doesn't mean you must do without what you need—or even what you want. Instead, these ideas help you spend less money, make your money go farther, or help you think before you buy. All of this helps you manage your money so you have enough for daily living and other spending.

17 Ideas for Living on Less

Some people just go with the flow when it comes to spending money. They don't plan their shopping, look for low prices, or think ahead about their child's changing needs. Eating out becomes a habit, as does picking up a few things at the convenience store on the corner.

One way to reduce expenses is to be smart about making your money go as far as possible. Here are some suggestions from other young parents that can really cut your expenses and keep money in your pocket:

1. Make a grocery list before you go shopping and stick with it. This helps limit impulse purchases, which can really add up. It also saves time both in the store and on return trips for stuff you forgot.

2. Shop sales and use coupons for the things you need.

3. Look at where you shop. Avoid buying diapers, groceries, health and beauty products—just about anything—at convenience stores or mini-marts. It may be convenient, but these shops often have higher prices than other stores.

4. Comparison shop—check around for the best prices on things you buy regularly.

5. Instead of going to the movies or a club, look for free entertainment in your community.

6. Don't rent videos you're not going to watch. And remember to return them on time.

7. Buy the store brand of canned and frozen foods, health and beauty products, and other items—not the national brands.

8. Shopping at discount stores like Target, Kmart, or Wal-Mart have good and bad sides. The good side is that many items cost less than elsewhere. The bad side is that these stores provide many temptations to buy things you don't need. Take a list and stick to it.

© Meld 2002 ◆ 612-332-7563

Sticking to the Budget

9. Careful meal planning can stretch your food dollar and avoid waste.

10. Consider the cost of convenience foods both in packaging as well as preparation. Is it cheaper to buy Cheerios in small boxes or to transfer some from the big box to smaller container for your diaper bag.

11. Consider the "dollar store" as a source of health and beauty aids. Again, though, "it's only a dollar" can really add up if you don't need it.

12. Compromise on your buying habits. If shoes are your thing, and you really want your child to have some cool shoes, consider buying less expensive jeans.

13. Trade services—are you good at doing hair or performing other services people need? If so, maybe you can trade haircuts for baby-sitting or some other activities.

14. Sometimes trade baby-sitting with a friend so you can go to the store alone for groceries or whatever. The whole experience will be less stressful and it will be easier to stick to your list.

15. You can often find like-new clothes, shoes, toys, and household goods at Goodwill, Salvation Army, Savers, garage sales, and other thrift stores.

16. Take your lunch to school or work.

More ideas:

_____
_____
_____
_____
_____
_____

© Meld 2002 ◆ 612-332-7563

Smart Money

Keeping on Top of My Money and Records

Even babies come with paperwork. One of the first official pieces of paper you will have after your baby is born is a birth certificate. Do you know where it is? What about your own birth certificate?

Growing up and becoming a parent leaves a long paper trail. Now is the time to get a handle on the paperwork and set up systems to keep track of it so you aren't buried under a blizzard of paper. It is very easy to get behind on your recordkeeping and it can take a lot of time and effort to get caught up.

It helps to stay on top of your money, too. Most of the money you receive from jobs, the government, and banks will be accompanied by paper. You need to understand these records, including paycheck stubs, bank records, credit reports, and more. You also need to control and record your money through checking and savings accounts.

Taking Care of Business

The first step in taking care of business is to set up an organizing system. You can do this in a big box, a file cabinet, a portable plastic file, a drawer of your dresser, or a notebook with pocket folders. You can use file folders with neat labels, hanging files, large envelopes with handwritten labels, or paper-clipped sets of papers. What matters most is that you understand the system and that you follow it! A few minutes to put something where it belongs now can save you hours later when looking for a copy of your child's immunization record, trying to file away three months worth of paper, preparing to work on your annual taxes, and so on.

The purpose of a file system is to keep similar papers and records together where you can quickly and easily find them. What follows are some of the basic records you will need to keep organized.

There are three very important documents all adults need:

1. **Birth certificate.** The official record of your birth, which shows where you were born, your parents' names and other vital statistics.

2. **Social security number.** This number identifies you in all government and tax records. You will need your social security number whenever you apply for a job.

3. **Drivers license or state photo ID card.** Carry this identification in your wallet or purse, but also make a copy for your file so you have the ID number in case you lose it.

Adults who are not American citizens need to have their resident papers, work permits, and other immigration documents showing they are in the U.S. legally. People born in other countries may or may not have birth certificates.

Taking Care of Business

Depending on your own circumstances, where you live, and services you receive, you may also have these records:
- adoption papers
- citizenship papers
- diplomas, education
- tribal identification certificates
- health insurance cards
- child support orders
- military discharge papers

> It is a major hassle—and takes time and money—to replace any of these official documents. Avoid this by keeping them in a safe place.

Both parents need to keep records for their child, too:
- Birth certificate.
- Declaration of paternity, if father is not on the birth certificate.
- Social security number. Parents must apply for a social security number for their child as identification.
- Immunization and other medical records. You will need to know when your child has been immunized before entering day care or school.
- A record of each parent's social security number and any other information (military discharge or tribal enrollment papers, for example) that affect the child's benefits.

Keep all these papers in a safe place and don't give anyone the original documents unless they are required. It is a good idea to have "notarized" copies on hand in case you need them. *Notarized* means that a notary public has certified that this is an accurate, true copy of the document or signature. You make the copies from the original and have both the original and copies available for the notary public to see. Notary publics are usually available at the court house, banks, and insurance agencies. There is usually a small fee to notarize something.

You will have paper records for many other parts of your life, too:
- health insurance and medical records
- other insurance

Taking Care of Business

- job related information (paycheck stubs, statement of benefits, description of benefits, union information, vacation/sick leave records…)
- financial records (check registers, canceled checks, loan documents…)
- education records (diplomas, certificates, records of grades…)
- tax records (state and federal tax returns…)
- bill receipts and payment records

Briefly outline your recordkeeping plan.

I will keep my records in…

_____
_____
_____
_____

These file headings make sense to me:

_____
_____
_____
_____

I will organize my files by…

_____
_____
_____
_____

Handling My Money

There are many ways to handle your money. You can operate completely on cash—keeping your money ready to spend, paying your bills in person, and writing down your spending. While this has some convenience, it is not a good idea to keep large amounts of cash on hand or in your wallet. It makes it really easy to spend it, lose it, or otherwise have it "fly" away! You can use money orders for bills and payments, but these have fees attached and you need to keep track of the receipts so you have a record of the money order. Wire transfer of funds by Western Union, for example, may be easy and convenient, but the fees for this service are quite large. The easiest way to keep track of your money is with a checking account.

Checking Account

A checking account has these advantages:
- It keeps your money safe.
- It lets you cash personal and payroll checks without a fee.
- A checking account allows you to write checks for your bills instead of paying cash or buying money orders. This means you will be able send payments through the mail. You may also choose to pay bills automatically by having the money withdrawn from your account and transferred to those to whom you make regular payments.
- It gives you a record of what you have spent.
- The canceled check provides you with proof of payment.

You set up a checking account at a bank, savings and loan, or credit union. There are many different types of accounts. Find one that is good for you by talking to someone at the bank or someone that you trust who knows about money. Consider these things when choosing an account:
- fees for the account
- minimum deposits (some banks require that you always have at least a set amount of money in your account)
- location of banks and branches

Handling My Money

- services offered
- helpfulness of staff
- other services available

Each bank will have its own form, but expect to have these documents and information with you to open an account:
- name, address, and phone number
- place of birth
- mother's maiden name (her last name at her birth)
- employer's name, address, and phone number
- social security number
- driver's license or state ID card

You must deposit money into each account you open. Banks vary on the amount, but it can be as little as $50-$100. Have this money with you.

When opening a checking account, the bank will give you the two parts of a checkbook: the blank checks and deposit slips, and the check register. You use the checks to pay for things. The deposit slips are for you to record the amount of cash and checks you deposit. You then record the checks you write and the money you deposit in the check register.

Some checks come with carbons. The carbon is the thin paper behind each check that acts as a record of the check. These carbons can be helpful reminders when balancing your checkbook. Often checking accounts with lower fees use this type of check because the bank doesn't return the canceled checks to you. Instead, you keep the carbons and if you need a copy of a canceled check as proof of payment, you request one from the bank (for a fee, of course!). The carbons also help if you forget to record a check in your check register—you have a record you can refer to right there!

Handling My Money

ATM Card

Your bank may offer you an ATM card (automated teller machine) to use to deposit and withdraw money from your checking or savings accounts, or to switch money from one account to another using an ATM computer terminal. This can be convenient, since ATM machines are in many places. Before using an ATM card, you should find out what fees may be involved. Be sure to record all ATM transactions and fees in your check register: withdrawals, deposits, and transfers will all affect your checking balance. Use the ATM machines cautiously. These "money machines" can be a temptation to keep your pocket filled with cash.

Handling My Money

Writing a Check

When you write a check, be sure to use permanent ink and write legibly. Fill in all the blanks and do not leave spaces at the beginning or ends of lines. If you leave spaces, someone could change the amount of your check.

Take a look at the completed check and then fill in the blank check for $13.67 for a prescription at Target.

Ineeda Workman
987 West East St.
Homeville, MN 55555

Date *August 1, 2002*

Pay to the Order of *ABC Grocery* $ *12.34*

Twelve & 34/100 ———————————— Dollars

Big Bank
Minneapolis, MN

For *food*   *Ineeda Workman*

Ineeda Workman
987 West East St.
Homeville, MN 55555

Date _____

Pay to the Order of _____ $ _____

_____ Dollars

Big Bank
Minneapolis, MN

For _____   _____

Handling My Money

Recording Your Checks

It is important to write down every check you write and every deposit you make in your check register. (Don't forget ATM transactions and any fees you may have been charged!)

> *Practice writing these transactions in the register below and keeping a running balance.*
> - Deposit $350 on April 29
> - $400 to Landlord Inc. for rent on May 1
> - $27.56 for baby formula at Food World on May 17
> - Groceries at Butterly's Foodstore for $17.53 on May 23
> - Deposit $350 on May 29
> - ATM withdrawal for $20 on May 30

Check no.	Date	Check issued to	Amount of Check	Amount of deposit	Balance
1021	2/1	VOID			75 89
1022	2/3	Butterly Foods	39 75		36 14
	2/7	Deposit		65 48	101 62

Each time you make a deposit, add it to your account balance. Subtract the amount of each check and ATM withdrawals and fees from the balance. The check register is the record of all these transactions.

© Meld 2002 ◆ 612-332-7563

Handling My Money

Filling Out a Deposit Slip

It is important to write down every check you write and every deposit you make in the check register.

> *Practice filling out a deposit slip by entering the following checks and cash on the blank deposit slip below.*
>
> Checks from:
> - Lucky Shoes $425.17 (paycheck)
> - Maria Guitierrez $12.00 (for baby-sitting)
> - Andre Davis $15.00 (birthday gift)
>
> Cash for:
> - $50 from child support

Checking Account Deposit Ticket				
Ineeda Workman **987 West East St.** **Homeville, MN 55555**	CASH	Currency		
		Coin		
	Checks			
Date _____	Total from other side			
	TOTAL			
	Less cash received			
Big Bank **Minneapolis, MN**	Net Deposit			

43-2948
284

Use other side for additional listing

Handling My Money

Balancing Your Checkbook

At the end of the month, the bank will send you a statement of your account. This shows all the checks you have written that have been cashed, the deposits made to the account, ATM transactions, and any fees. It may include your canceled checks, depending on the type of account you have. You need to balance—or reconcile—your check register with the bank statement to see if you both agree about how much money is in your account. Often on the back of the statement is a form you can use to do this.

The bank statement you receive might look similar to this:

Your name Your address		Account No. Statement Date	
Total amount checks	Total amount deposits	Balance this statement	Balance last statement
61.04	154.36	169.21	75.89
CHECKS	DEPOSITS	BALANCE	DATE
39.75		36.14	2/5
	65.48	101.62	2/8
21.29		80.33	2/20
	88.88	169.21	2/21

Handling My Money

Here's how to balance your checkbook with the bank's statement:

1. Take out your check register, bank statement, pencil, paper, and calculator.

2. Compare your check register amounts for deposits and checks to the amounts on the bank statement. Mark off each one as you see it's correct.

3. Note deposits made since the bank statement was prepared. Add these to the bank statement balance.

4. Write down any checks outstanding—those you have written since the bank statement was prepared or which haven't yet been cashed. Add these up. Then subtract the amount from the new balance you figured above. This is Total 1.

5. Note any fees/charges from the bank (service charges, check printing charges, etc.)

6. Subtract the fees/charges from the register balance. This is Total 2.

Checking account reconciliation form

Outstanding Checks			Use the area below to reconcile your account.			
No.	Dollars	Cents				
			Bank balance on statement	_____	Register balance	_____
			Add deposits not shown on this statement	_____	Service charges	_____
					Subtotal	_____
					+ Interest	_____
			Total deposits	_____	TOTAL 2	_____
			Subtotal	_____		
			Subtract total of outstanding checks	_____	TOTAL 1 should equal TOTAL 2	
	Total		TOTAL 1	_____		

If your totals are not the same, go back and look for a mistake. Banks do make mistakes, but you probably will make some, too. If you can't get it to add up, don't panic. Try again. If you still can't get it to balance, call the bank or go talk to them for help in getting it right.

Don't ignore problems with your balance. You need to have an accurate record so you don't write checks for more than you have. "Bounced" checks mean charges from your bank and often from the stores where you wrote the check. These charges are expensive and can make a *big* dent in your budget.

It's a good idea, if possible, to have a savings account where you have a checking account. If you have both accounts, bank fees may be less. It is easier to transfer money from one account to another, too, and you can often do it by phone or ATM.

Saving My Money

There are many reasons to save money:

- for an emergency—car breakdown, illness, etc.
- for a rainy day fund
- to help you reach your education/training goals
- to help you get where you want to be in life
- to help send your child to college or to pay for other opportunities for your child—music lessons, a bike, summer camp, etc.
- to buy your own home—this can be a great strategy for investing your money wisely!

List some reasons you have to save money based on your goals.

_____
_____
_____
_____
_____
_____
_____
_____
_____

Saving My Money

It Pays to Save

Saving money pays off. When you put your money in a savings account, it earns interest.

Interest is a wonderful thing. It is a fee that the bank pays you to use your money. When you deposit your money in a savings account, it doesn't just sit around in piles in a bank vault. The bank uses that money to make loans (for a fee, also called interest) to other people and businesses. As long as your money is in the bank, they will pay interest. This can add up.

Savings accounts earn "compound interest." This means you earn interest today on the interest you earned yesterday. Each time interest is added to your savings, the new total is used to figure your interest the next time. Interest can be compounded daily, monthly, quarterly, or annually. The more often, the better.

Let's say you put some money every week into a savings account with 2% interest, compounded daily. What will it add up to?

	After 3 Yrs.	After 5 Yrs.
$5 per week x .02 interest =	$ 803.65	$1,366.76
$10 per week x .02 interest =	$1,607.30	$2,733.51

Not bad for leaving your money in the bank. It does take patience and determination not to take the money out of savings to reach these numbers, but you can do it.

Saving My Money

Set up a savings account at a bank or credit union as soon as you can. Don't "save" money under your bed or in your drawer. It is too easy to lose it or spend it. A savings account

- keeps your money safe
- provides money for "rainy days"
- reminds you to save each pay period
- helps keep track of your savings goals
- shows the bank and others that you can manage money
- establishes credit
- earns money through interest

With your savings account you may receive a passbook, which is the record of your deposits, withdrawals, and the interest paid on your account. Take this with you to the bank whenever you make a deposit or withdrawal from your savings account.

Saving My Money

Your Savings

Decide how much money you will save each week from your pay. Some people recommend saving at least 10% of your pay, but that isn't always possible when you are just starting out. Don't worry if you can't save a lot at once. Start small and work your way to larger amounts.

The saving habit is an important one to develop. And, if you save, your money will add up. Take a look.

Think about what you are saving for and how much you can put away. Here is one way to figure out how to reach your goal.

> Say you want to save $520 in one year (52 weeks):
>
> $520 ÷ 52 weeks = $10 per week (the amount you need to save to reach your goal)

Once you set up your savings plan, stick to it. Make some rules for yourself about when and why you will spend your savings. This will help you spend your savings wisely.

Ask yourself questions like these before spending your savings:
- Is this a real emergency?
- Do I really need this item?
- How else could I use my savings if I didn't spend it on this?
- If I spend my savings now, will I regret it next week or next month?
- Will I still want to spend this money as much if I just waited for a few hours to make sure?

> Once you are comfortable managing your money and you understand how money "grows" through savings, you may want to learn about investing your money. Investing is another way to make your money grow. There are various ways to invest—in the stock market or mutual funds, for example. You can learn more by taking a class, reading books, or talking with an investment professional or people you know who invest.

Saving My Money

Ways to Save Money

There are many different ways to start saving money. Here are some examples, but you probably know of others that would also work for you:

- Put away a dollar a day or save all your change in a jar. After a few months, add it up and take it to the bank to put in your savings account.
- If you get a raise, put that amount into your savings account and live on what you were making before the raise.
- If you receive an earned income credit, a tax refund, or other refund, put it in your savings.
- Skip a fast-food meal (eat at home) and put the money you would have spent in savings.
- Give up or cut down on smoking, snacks, or whatever, and put that money in savings.

Other ideas I can use to start saving money:
_____
_____
_____
_____
_____

If an emergency means you need to use your savings, you can be proud you were prepared. But keep on saving—always!

The Check's in the Mail: Setting Up a Bill Paying System

It is important to pay your bills on time. This establishes a good credit history for you if you want to move or take out a loan—you are on record as paying your bills. Some companies, especially credit card companies, apply interest and/or late fees to bills, which add up in a hurry and are a real waste of money. Setting up a bill paying system will help you pay your bills when they are due.

You can pay bills in person by cash or check, or by mailing a check or money order. Each of these methods has advantages. If you pay bills in person, you can do it on the day the bill is due, giving yourself a little more control over cash flow. If you pay in cash, be sure to get an official receipt for the payment and file it with your bill receipts.

Paying by mail is most convenient, but you need to have a checking account or purchase money orders. NEVER SEND CASH IN THE MAIL! Mail the bill a few days before it's due so it gets there on time. You will also need stamps because the post office won't deliver unstamped mail.

Get organized!

- Find a box, expandable folder, or some other container to keep all your paperwork, files, and supplies organized. Put everything you need in the container, including pens and pencils, envelopes, postage stamps, calculator, etc. When your bills come in the mail, open the envelopes and record the date due and amount on the outside of the envelopes. Then file the bills in the box by the date they need to be paid.

- If you use money orders, make a list of the amount of each one you need, and who it should be made out to. Try to make one trip to buy all the money orders. This will save time. You need cash to buy money orders. Each one you buy will have a fee. Shop around to find the place with the lowest fee. Fill out the money orders as soon as you get them. Money orders are like cash and anyone can spend them if you lose them before filling them out. Be sure to keep the stub that comes with the money order—it is your receipt.

The Check's in the Mail: Setting Up a Bill Paying System

- Set up a regular time each week to pay bills and review your budget. With your box of supplies, and your checkbook and check register or money orders at hand, write out your bills. On each check or money order stub, write the account number or other information on the line at the bottom left corner, for example: "Rent, May 2002." This will help you remember what the check was for and identifies your account with the company so you get credited correctly for paying the bill.

    On the bill receipt, write the date paid and the number of the check number or money order you used to pay the bill. If you get a written receipt (for example, for your rent), write the date and check number on it so you have that information.

- Keep your bill receipts for at least one year. Keep canceled checks, check registers, and money order stubs indefinitely. Having these records can help in case you later have a problem with a bill. File them in your filing system.

- Get into the habit of paying your bills regularly and on time. This helps establish good credit.

In The End…

Once you've done all the activities in this workbook, go back to the **Dollars and Sense** chapter and retake the "Smart About My Money" assessment. How much have you learned about your money? Are you surprised by how smart you are about your money?

Managing your money isn't a once-a-week thing. You really do have to keep on top of things so you know how much money you have, can pay your bills on time, and have money for your savings.

Learn all you can about money. As you learn and understand more about it, you can look ahead to investing, having more control, and gaining the satisfaction of knowing you're smart about your money. You will have taken a great step towards caring for your child and building a strong foundation for your family's future.

parenting that works

Order Form			
Qty.	Title	$ Each	Total
	Money Matters	$7.95	

Subtotal _____

Shipping & handling _____

MN residents add 6.5% sales tax _____

Total _____

Shipping & Handling

For orders subtotaling:
Up to $25 $5.00
$25.01 to $75 $7.00
$75.01 to $150 $9.00
Over $150   8% of subtotal

Please call for Air Delivery Services and International Delivery pricing.

All orders must be prepaid.

Most orders are shipped within 2 days from receipt of order (7 to 9 delivery days).

Call for quantity discounts!

Send book(s) to:

Name _____

Agency _____

Street address _____

City _____

State _____ Zip _____

Telephone _____

Email _____

Method of Payment:

☐ Check or money order payable to Meld

☐ Visa   ☐ MasterCard   ☐ American Express

Account No. _____

Exp. Date _____

Signature _____

Mail to:
Meld ◆ 219 North Second Street ◆ Suite 200
Minneapolis, MN 55401

You can also order by phone, fax or on our website!

612-332-7563   612-344-1959 (fax)   www.meld.org

Order Form

Qty.	Title	$ Each	Total
	Money Matters	$7.95	

Subtotal _____

Shipping & handling _____

MN residents add 6.5% sales tax _____

Total _____

Shipping & Handling

For orders subtotaling:

Up to $25	$5.00
$25.01 to $75	$7.00
$75.01 to $150	$9.00
Over $150	8% of subtotal

Please call for Air Delivery Services and International Delivery pricing.

All orders must be prepaid.

Most orders are shipped within 2 days from receipt of order (7 to 9 delivery days).

Call for quantity discounts!

Send book(s) to:

Name _____

Agency _____

Street address _____

City _____

State _____ Zip _____

Telephone _____

Email _____

Method of Payment:

☐ Check or money order payable to Meld

☐ Visa   ☐ MasterCard   ☐ American Express

Account No. _____

Exp. Date _____

Signature _____

Mail to:

Meld ◆ 219 North Second Street ◆ Suite 200
Minneapolis, MN 55401

You can also order by phone, fax or on our website!

612-332-7563   612-344-1959 (fax)   www.meld.org